Unleashing Your Full Potential!

....

Remove the Obstacles that Hinder Your Progress and Unlock Your True Potential for Limitless Growth. Empowering Your Journey to Happiness.

•

EMILY KENDALL

....
Copyright © 2021 Emily Kendall
All rights reserved.

CONTENTS

Preface	5
Introduction	7
Chapter 1: In the Search of Your Best Self	15
Chapter 2: In the Search of Inspiration	23
Chapter 3: In the Search of Motivation	31
Chapter 4: In the Search of Creativity	39
Chapter 5: In the Search of Spiritual Growth	49
Chapter 6: In the Search of Self-Actualization	55
Chapter 7: In the Search of Inner Peace & Understanding	65
Chapter 8: In the Search of Relieving Mental Health Blocks	75
Chapter 9: In the Search of Relieving Stress, Anxiety & Indecision	81
Chapter 10: In the Search of Confidence & Self-Awareness	89
Chapter 11: In the Search of The Process	107
Conclusion: Achieved Height	111

Preface

"Never let life impede on your ability to manifest your dreams. Dig deeper into your dreams and deeper into yourself and believe that anything is possible, and make it happen."

~ Corin Nemec

In bringing this book to life, the whole intention behind it is to help you, the reader, discover new and exciting ways to achieve greater heights than ever before. The sections that follow will break several steps down to help you get there much quicker and painlessly. There are many ways that you can get to where you want to be in life; discovering height and heightened awareness is only one of them.

Once you have the basics down and you know what to do to motivate yourself moving forward, the rest will fall into place and life and your dreams will just open up for you. The key is to direct all your focus, energy, and attention to your goals for you to discover health, happiness, and a life of peace and joy.

May you find what you are looking for and more.

Introduction

"If one advances confidently in the direction of his dreams, and endeavors to live the life which he has imagined, he will meet with a success unexpected in common hours."

~Henry David Thoreau

If I were to ask you to give me the definition of what height means to you, or the highest place you can think of, I could almost put money on it that most of you will identify with Mount Everest or somewhere similar. Everest stands at an impressive almost 30,000 feet above sea level. You may be wondering what this has to do with being able to elevate your life. The answer to your question is that it has everything to do with it.

We have from the very beginning strived to conquer heights, to scale what some think is unattainable; this search of height has been with us and will continue to be. We now turn this pursuit inwards to strive to conquer within us this same height metaphorically. When it comes to Everest itself, it has always been certain that it is man versus the mountain or man versus nature. Just as you may need to learn to overcome certain physical and mental challenges in order for you to achieve the things that you dream of, you need to focus on being able to elevate your life.

Before we begin on this journey, it is recommended that you find yourself a notebook where you can record the answers to some of the questions asked or jot down notes of ideas that may come to mind as we begin to work through the elevation process. Are you ready? Let us begin!

The experience of gazing out into the distance from vast heights allows an individual to contemplate their very existence and put themselves into a state that truly expands their world view and consciousness. It is from this perspective that I would like to invite each of you to join me as we discover how you, too, can learn to elevate your life.

What does it mean to "elevate your life"? The word elevate is described by the Merriam- Webster dictionary as being four different things. Let us consider what each of these is:

1. The first is "to lift up or make higher by raising."
2. Next is "to raise in rank or status."
3. The third is "to improve morally, intellectually, or culturally."
4. And finally, "to raise the spirits" (Merriam-Webster, 2021).

The ultimate goal of the book is to help you become inspired, to help you raise your spirits so that you are able to apply all these definitions of elevating oneself to your life and your search of height.

In the sections that follow, we are going to consider each of these four areas and how they can be applied to our lives, to lift us up to where we need to be. Before we get into the heart of what *Unleashing Your Full Potential* is all about, let us try the following exercise: Close your eyes and imagine being transported to your own secret place where you can look out before you and see vistas upon vistas, from rolling hills to distant mountains. Here you can sit and watch a glorious morning sunrise or a multi-palette sunset at the end of a busy day. You are completely alone; it is just you, the mountain, and a magnificent view. You are feeling relaxed, content, and as though you are ready to take on the rest of the world.

- What are some of the sounds that you hear?
- Is there a slight chill in the air that you are beginning to feel?
- Or can you feel the sun on your face as you close your eyes to enjoy the moment?
- Can you smell anything that is distinct—maybe there happens to be a forest near the precipice you have chosen?
- How far can you see?
- What do you see all around you?
- Most importantly, what do you feel?

Remember each of these feelings because this is definitely going to be something you want to recreate. This image needs to be seared into your brain so fully that you can mentally transport yourself to this place whenever you need to. During the actual process, you are going to physically look for a real physical environment that meets all the criteria necessary, but for now, visualize what this will look like.

This is where the notebook or journal could come in handy. Make some notes about how you are expecting to feel as and when you physically find your very own personal spot where you can survey the territory from a physical position of height.

Since the beginning of time, we know that mankind has been chasing these things. All you have to do is consider history, how towers were constructed in order to try and reach the heavens. Consider the pharaohs and the pyramids in Egypt—each of them was built with considerable height in mind. You can just picture the Sphinx and other monuments they built to honor their leaders and their gods.

More modern architecture has pushed the boundaries, with each country aiming for bragging rights for having the tallest of skyscrapers or tourist attractions with observation decks of marvel. Think of places like the Statue of Liberty or the Eiffel Tower. Each of these structures has been built with a view for being able to enjoy the magnificence of either Manhattan or Paris. Even more modern than this, we can travel to places in Dubai or the United Arab Emirates, home to some of the tallest skyscrapers.

It is not only a result of physical structures but also man himself that wants to push the envelope and boundaries of what is humanly possible, making things that were once believed to be impossible possible. This is where our focus is going to take us. We are going to literally consider how, through actual physical elevation, you can alter the trajectory of your own life by changing your attitude, changing how you perceive the world, and changing yourself in the process.

You have been aiming for things that are at a much higher level than what you are at currently. Chasing new heights can be quite literal, or it can be something as simple as learning new skills or building on those skills you already have. The goal is to improve on your talents and abilities and everything you choose to do with your life.

There is a reason why homes with majestic views are always pricier than those constructed in areas where there is overcrowding and where homes are one on top of another. You end up paying for the view that you get to enjoy. Wherever you go, it happens to be the same.

In any city in the world, the higher the skyscraper with magnificent views of the city, the greater the cost per square footage. Imagine being able to look out of your corner office window in awe and amazement at everything happening below you. This is where the hefty price tag comes in. Remember what they say about location being everything. It is no different whether you are referring to your office space or where you happen to be situated in life.

In this short book, we are going to uncover some of the things you could be doing to elevate yourself to new and exciting heights that will improve every area of your life. We will also cover how to achieve self-awareness and confidence by developing your inner peace through inspirational spiritual growth and motivation. Here you will become empowered to formulate new habits, break old ones that hold you back, and develop the capacity to recharge and reset yourself whenever you feel the need. This is a never-ending quest for betterment.

This is not something that is passive; instead, it is a guide that you can begin putting into practice almost immediately to make the most out of your life. In the pages that follow, we are going to literally focus on height and the feeling that one gets from being able to observe the world from this completely new angle.

This really does not matter whether you choose to view the world from a mountainous region that is close to you. Maybe you are living in a suburban area, and the best you can do is get to the top of a high-rise building or tower. That is quite okay. What you are aiming for is being able to look outward with the view to sensing the vast expanse of the universe all around you.

If you cannot manage to find any of these places, try settling for lying on your back on a blanket under the stars as you view them from our perspective. This will truly give you a big picture view of the majesty of nature and where you are trying to get to in your life. Strive for finding somewhere higher since this is always better. More importantly, do what you can to live *Unleashing Your Full Potential! Remove the Obstacles that Hinder Your Progress and Unlock Your True Potential for Limitless Growth. Empowering Your Journey to Happiness.*

.

Chapter 1:
In the Search of Your Best Self

"Owning our story and loving ourselves through that process is the bravest thing that we'll ever do."

~ Brené Brown

As we work through this process, I am going to try and break things down as much as possible so they are easily understood and even easier to apply to your daily life. I'm sure that we've all faced those dark and dreary days where you just lie there wondering, what is it all for? Why are you here? And is there a purpose to anything? I can virtually see you nodding your head because I know I've certainly been there.

I often wonder whether our contribution to society is worth it. Does it really matter? The most important contribution to society we can make is to our individual self-development and growth—it is only when we elevate ourselves we can then help others do the same. I'll be honest with you; these kinds of questions are the ones that keep you up at night. They're the ones that often lead to some serious soul-searching where deep introspection takes place—where we try and find the answers to some of life's toughest questions—the questions worth pondering over.

Self-Awareness

Before you can get to answering these questions about yourself, don't you agree that you'd really need to know who you are first? Gaining some insight into self-awareness is how you manage to get through this one. So, before we begin our ascent up this mountain on this journey of ours, let's stop and consider exactly who we are for a while.

According to Neil Blumenthal,

"Self-awareness is a trait–or maybe 'practice' is the more accurate way to put it– that everyone can always improve at. It is part emotional intelligence, part perceptiveness, part critical thinking. It means knowing your weaknesses, of course, but it also means knowing your strengths and what motivates you."

This single quotation explains so perfectly what self-awareness is that there's no real need to go into too much detail.

Spending time alone with nature, preferably at a height, to really draw you into the vastness of it all allows one to realize this vastness is within us. This presents us an excellent opportunity for contemplating who we are as an individual. We can use this energy to grow; we allow it to help us consider what our strengths, talents, or gifts are that we bring to the world, as well as our limitations or weaknesses. We need to know this so we can constantly attempt to play toward our strengths and talents. Our limitations and weaknesses are areas that we will now recognize as needing work.

It's the ability to focus inwardly and truly assess your true nature from a psychological perspective. This is something that happens to occur mainly on a subconscious rather than a conscious level. The secret to becoming self-aware stems from your ability to focus.

Research shows that we are born with an acute sense of self-awareness which is what probably keeps us alive for the first few years of our lives. We are sensitive to the touch of others. We know when we have a need to be met, such as hunger, pain, fatigue, or being changed. How do we know that infants have this sense? Quite simply because they communicate with their primary caregiver that this is what is necessary.

As we get older, we begin relying on ourselves and focus on being able to express ourselves to those around us more. So, what happens when there's a bit of a disconnect in this department? Psychologists have divided self-awareness into separate sections:

Public

This makes us behave in a certain way because we are aware that we are being watched and possibly even assessed or evaluated. Because of this, our behavior is likely to change. We are often more inclined to behave in ways that are contrary to our true human nature. We do this because we want to be seen to be socially acceptable. There could be a negative aspect when it comes to this type of awareness. An additional negative aspect can be altering your life to please others and suppressing yourself to fit in. Where we battle with crowds, we may not like being the center of attention or being in the public spotlight. In this instance, we may even begin to experience feelings that display anxiety or a degree of nervousness. This stress is caused when we consider what the perception of others really is and how we fit into that mold and bend to it when we shouldn't.

Private

You may find yourself responding in a certain way that is not displayed to those around you. An example of this could be feeling extremely anxious about facing your driving examination or a medical appointment where you are nervous about the diagnosis or outcome. You are not necessarily going to openly vocalize how you are feeling about it. Private self-awareness is how we respond to certain stimuli that are around us.

Self-Consciousness

When you are overly self-aware, this could result in behaving in a way where you are so self-conscious of every action. You automatically assume that you are under the microscope, that people are staring at you, and you are being judged. The result of this is often social awkwardness or intense nervousness. For many, this could just be a temporary thing, while for others, it is a permanent disorder (Cherry & Goldman, 2020).

We need to be self-aware in the world in order to be able to understand ourselves and others. While you are contemplating the beauty around you, consider your place in the universe. How majestic you truly are, and what a wonderful time it is to be alive.

Think about which of these three areas you fall into when it comes to self-awareness.

Are there things that you need to do to improve? *(Hint—we can always do more to improve; that is one of the secrets to pursuing height—to become the best version of yourself.)*

Becoming Your Best Self

Spending some alone time with your journal, a pen, and your thoughts, consider each of the following questions as far as living your best self is concerned.

- Shouldn't living your best life be fun?
- Are you doing everything you can do to better yourself?
- How do you manage to live your best life?
- Does it mean you need a lot of friends?

- What does living your best life even mean?

- Are you placing limitations on yourself?

- Does it mean that you need to be wealthy?

- Do you need to live in a mansion?

- Do you need to be smarter than everyone else?

- Do you need to have excessive fancy 'stuff'?

These 10 questions should be more than enough to get yourself started. Jot them down in your journal as you receive insights into each one of them while you're meditating on your mountain. Allow your thoughts to flow freely and write whatever comes to mind without passing judgment or feeling that things need to be absolutely correct.

Nobody but you can define who you really are as a person. This is why this exercise is so vitally important. This should definitely be the very first thing that you tackle so you gain a much better understanding of where you are on this life journey—what you ought to be doing with yourself and what the right way is for you to begin an inner dialogue with yourself.

While yes, although you are looking for limitations and areas that you need to improve, this should not be your sole focus of this exercise. Instead, it should be spent trying to get to know yourself a little better. Some of these questions may be hard to ask and answer honestly. We don't want to be seen in a bad light with anyone, least of all ourselves. There are, however, positives to gain from being able to see ourselves in a bad light. We can realize what aspects of our life need to be improved on. This is an important aspect of self- elevation, of growth. (The real problem is when you think that there's nothing you can improve on.)

The problem with us agonizing over who we really are as individuals is the fact that we are often much harder on ourselves than anyone else would be. We judge ourselves differently from the way anyone else would judge us. We see faults and flaws within our character, in the person who stares back at us in the mirror. We often beat ourselves up incessantly over things that have happened in the past that should actually just be left there. Let the past die, forgive yourself, and move on. We take upon ourselves the responsibility to improve on our faults and flaws, to stand tall through it all.

There are constant thoughts running through our heads that are critical about everything we do. It takes a long time and a lot of practice to be able to silence these inner voices that do nothing but berate us and make us feel unimportant. Part of the process we are going to go through is to try and answer each of these questions, but it all needs to start right at the beginning, with YOU!

Chapter 2:
In the Search of Inspiration

"If you are working on something that you really care about, you don't have to be pushed. The vision pulls you."

~ Steve Jobs

This is possibly one of the most challenging areas to be able to motivate someone toward change because what is inspirational to you is not necessarily inspirational to me. We each differ, and because of this, our requirements are almost as unique. We need to accept that along with growth, adversity in the form of obstacles and challenges will occur almost naturally.

How do you get into the right frame of mind so you are constantly driven toward whatever goal you have deemed as being worthy enough to earn your attention? Some of the greatest challenges that we face when we are dealing with remaining positive and being able to live our best lives possible can be achieved through some of these tips, tools, and techniques:

One of the first things that people will often discuss with you is where your current priorities lie. Are you focusing your efforts and attention on whatever happens to be in the pile of your things to do, or are you prioritizing? Working with things that you have prioritized, what are your key criteria for prioritizing each of these things? A larger question we can ask is, are you prioritizing yourself and your growth?

Are you even factoring your passion into how you are prioritizing those things you would like to accomplish in your life? If not, you need to be able to learn pretty quickly to try and fill your life with those things that you are genuinely passionate about, rather than merely choosing to go along simply for the ride.

One of the biggest challenges when it comes to "living your best life" is whether or not you can clearly define what that life looks like and what you want it to look like. If you aren't doing those things that you are genuinely passionate about, life is going to begin becoming extremely boring and tedious indeed, which only leads to regrets.

Where can we find the necessary motivation we need to complete the goals that we have now managed to identify?

How do we change things so we end up working mainly on those goals we are passionate about?

Maybe you feel that there's so much more that you could and should be doing. Another game-changer when it comes to the goals you are working toward is measuring how busy you are and how much you can manage in the time you have left (without forcing burnout).

To discover each of those things that will motivate you toward really being able to live your best life and not one of mediocrity is by placing all your attention, emphasis, and effort on those things that you are genuinely interested in. Everything you prioritize should be listed according to two things—what is it that you would really love to be doing, and are these things right at the top of your list of priorities for the day?

Restore Balance

In order to accomplish great things within yourself and externally, it is very important to be balanced emotionally, physically, mentally, and spiritually. The conflict within us can easily be manifested back to us from the outside, in the form of out-of-control situations, personal conflicts, and/or a general state of discord. Many people talk about examples such as work/life balance; however, I would argue that without internal balance, your life cannot begin to take on any semblance of coordination. It will always be a struggle of juggling everything, just being moments away from dropping the ball at any moment. There is a time and place to make necessary sacrifices to achieve something else. This internal balance allows you to make as right a decision as possible at the right time.

Do you truly understand what is meant by personal growth? It is literally striving to live your life better today than you did yesterday. The end result is always to become a better person than you currently are by doing whatever is necessary in order to achieve your objectives. This is usually accomplished by working on different aspects or areas of your life.

Some of these areas could include being able to further your education, gaining new insights into life through different experiences, or changing your current mindset. Everyone has their very own reason for wanting to achieve personal growth, and it is usually something that is very personal. It may be as simple as wanting to become a more well-rounded individual or looking to do it for a very specific reason.

If you are in a position where you don't know where to go or how to get there because you're simply feeling 'stuck,' you are not alone. There are countless people who feel the same. However, it is the ones who set upon themselves the purpose to grow and push beyond mediocrity, to achieve within, the elevation they seek.

Personal growth may be something of a necessity if you've experienced a problem and need to learn different coping mechanisms to be able to move on. Often these are the toughest challenges to go through, but they provide you with the most unique opportunities to develop and strengthen multiple areas of your life, making you a much stronger, well-rounded individual by the end of the process. I would like to add a quote that has helped me throughout the years to understand my failures or challenges and how they provide learning opportunities. "The greatest teacher, failure is"—Yoda.

All of this can be tied back to your experience that you have at your perfect spot where you can contemplate the universe and your place in it. It's all a question of being able to put things into perspective—one that is so much bigger than you or I could ever begin to imagine. Use your time in your elevated position (or through stargazing) as a means of discovering what it is that you need to be doing in order to feel fulfilled as a human being.

Don't be too surprised if what you feel will often seem like 'aha' moments, or you may easily feel like you're being shown your very own private epiphany by the universe. As you keep noticing and taking mental notes of these epiphanies, moments of creativity, and/or synchronicity, they will begin to happen more and more frequently. You can come down from your mountain with a completely different outlook than the one you had when you ventured to your spot. It's expansive views like this that get people to totally reevaluate their lives. They want to become something better than they currently are, and it's through these high-level meditations where you will be able to feel the answers flow into you.

What are some of the ways that you can improve your life? Please understand that this is your very own personal story. While I can guide you through some of the processes that we know work, you may want to replace them with something else that's already working for you in your life. That's perfectly fine. The most important thing is that you at least attempt some of these. I can promise you that the least you will get from it is an amazing view and some quiet time, and the most you can get is still to be determined, the awakening of a whole new perspective waiting to be acted on.

Feed Your Mind

The process of feeding your mind can take shape through reading, a very simple yet powerful habit to add to your quest for elevation. The act of going through this book now, I hope, will bring you the inspiration you need to further your search for knowledge. The sheer amount of material out there can make your head spin. It is important to get a basic grasp on what interests you, to start, and pursue that; as you do, more information will come to you that is needed for you to read at that time. As your perception grows, more information will continue to come. It is a cycle you develop and grow with.

Whether you are looking to increase your productivity in the workplace, to improve communication skills across all your relationships, wanting to increase your bottom-line earnings, or whatever the subject matter, you are certain to find some excellent titles available. As you go through each of these books, make use of a journal to compile the most motivating and inspirational pieces of knowledge for yourself. This, as time goes on, will be worth re-reading. It will be a compilation of the most important information that resonated with you; use it, learn from it, and it will always be with you.

This is one of the most important perspectives. The notes that you make must be cohesive and make sense within your own mind. The goal of this exercise is that all these notes are going to act to increase your level of motivation as you move on to other topics.

Your notes are your personal understanding of concepts that are meant for you alone. Your motivation will further grow, and your inspiration along with it. Allow yourself to feel out those books that you are drawn to, as they may be just what you need at the time and are what's right for you. Ask people you admire, who seem to have things all together, to recommend books that they have read themselves. Make a list because I can guarantee you that if they are into personal development, there won't only be one book that they've received inspiration from. This is not a singular process, but it is something you continue to do throughout this process of your growth, furthering your mind's elevation.

In further sections, we are going to talk about how to incorporate this particular habit into your life by changing just a couple of small things daily.

Chapter 3:
In the Search of Motivation

"What lies behind you and what lies in front of you, pales in comparison to what lies inside of you."

~ Ralph Waldo Emerson

Becoming motivated and staying that way is one of the many challenges of many people in today's society. No matter how positive we normally are, there's always that possibility of sliding into a rut or feeling the uncomfortable grips of a slump that's threatening to hold you back and possibly even derail whatever positive thoughts or emotions you happened to have. It doesn't matter whether you are a master of positive thinking and positive action; even some of the world's greatest individuals still go through times when they are feeling down and despondent.

It's not so much how many times you get knocked back down again, as the number of times you insist on standing back up again that will count. So, how do you go about this even when it feels like you are the only one who is experiencing this at the time? Are you the only one ever to be challenged by the discouragement monster? Or, occasionally, when reality sinks in, do you realize you're not quite as far as you would like to be? Understand that you are where you need to be in life, and there is a lesson that needs to be solved in order to move on.

There are times when we just feel that change is impossible, and it looks like it's going to be a lot of hard work. There's no doubt about it—any and all change that needs to take place is always hard work. We need to totally experience a complete metamorphosis for change to be worthwhile. And that means experiencing some pain. It means by going through some difficulties, which are the refining fires of the individual, we come out stronger and forged from the experience.

Maybe they aren't even in the form of an actual physical experience. Maybe your difficulty comes in the form of a challenging relationship with someone in the workplace or a challenging relationship with a member of your family. And yes, even the most successful people can still experience a whole host of challenges and difficulties.

Why do we need these experiences so desperately? The truth is that we all need to learn what it takes to get up again once we've been knocked down. For many of us, this is especially a time for learning and growth. All we have to do is to consider nature—how as soon as babies have reached a certain stage of growth and development, they get left to fend for themselves. Mother birds kick their babies out of the nest, and those little babies must either fly or fall. Both the lion and lioness will teach their cubs how to hunt, but pretty soon, they need to fend for themselves.

There's a common thread that runs through each of these examples. Lessons are taught or experienced, and once these have been handed down for a while, it certainly becomes a case of sink or swim. The offspring are either going to make it in the wild, or the wild is going to prove to be a desperate experience for them.

If you haven't picked up on this message just yet, it's meant to help you understand that even in nature, there comes a time where the spoon-feeding of assistance comes to an end and only the toughest actually survive. It may sound harsh, but you need to be able to become resilient and self-confident in your own abilities to be able to make it in the unforgiving world out there. Some other ways of increasing your levels of motivation when you happen to be feeling down are as follows:

Accountability Partner

Find someone to agree to be your accountability partner. You will then need to share almost every aspect of your goals with them. An accountability partner is going to demand that you report your progress regularly. Having an accountability partner means that it is your responsibility to communicate with them. Their role is to try and keep you motivated and moving toward achieving your goal. It isn't their responsibility to actually ensure that you are doing what you are supposed to be doing. You should accept this responsibility for yourself.

Create Anticipation

One of the best ways to create anticipation is through forward planning. Anticipation is very difficult to try and create immediately–if you want to begin working on a goal immediately. Whereas, by delaying the start date for your goal by a week or a month, you can physically add it to your calendar. As you begin counting down the days, your sense of anticipation will grow, and by the time your start date comes around, you will be ready and willing to do whatever it takes to get going with your goal.

Identify Only One Thing

Often when we feel like we're heading toward a funk, one of the best things to do is to assess or reassess where we are right now. How much are you trying to do? Are you sitting with just too much going on right now? I'm sure that we can all identify with times when you feel like you want to stop the world from spinning so you can just get off. Stop for a couple of seconds and reassess each item. Prioritize what needs to be done but then give just one thing that you have going on your complete and utter focus and attention. Work on a single project. Don't move from the project until such time as you have completed it. Once you have successfully managed to check this off your list, move onto your next goal until this can clearly be scratched from your to-do list as well. Work through each of these goals this way, remembering to only work on one thing at a time. Anything more than this, and you're headed back down that slippery slope of feeling completely out of control again.

Look for Excitement

Although this may come across as being an obvious answer, you would be surprised how few people are actually excited about their goals. If you aren't excited, how could you ever become truly motivated? If you find that your goal is not able to make you excited, then it may be time for you to find another goal to work on. Trying to force yourself to become excited about a goal is going to frustrate you and the process further. It won't motivate you or move you toward achieving your goal; instead, you will probably find excuses as to why you cannot achieve the goal.

Make a Public Declaration

Let your friends and family into whatever goals you are aiming for. They will become your cheerleaders and your monitors. They will motivate you to get up and do it whenever you feel like giving in.

Make It Visual

You can easily do this by either writing out your goal in large letters or finding an actual visual representation of what you want to achieve. Be sure that these are pasted all over your home or your office, on your bathroom mirror, or anywhere you spend a significant amount of time in a day.

Smaller Is Better

Rather start small on things that you know you can do and with achievements you know will produce positive results. Focus on small improvements daily. Look at areas that you can improve by just 1% every day. Implement this for at least a month. As you continue to grow and develop, keep improving by 1% every day. This way, you can celebrate each small victory as and when it occurs. Think about how you would conquer Mount Everest. You wouldn't just arrive there and start climbing. No! You would spend many months, if not a year or so, training to ensure you were in peak physical condition to make the journey. You would even concentrate on all the right equipment you may need to make the trip.

Tenacity

This means being able to stick to each of the goals that you set for yourself and that you're working on. Do this no matter what happens, through good times and bad. If you want to develop the habit of working toward your goals, then it's important that you understand that you won't always be working under the ideal circumstances. This is fine, as long as you keep at it without giving up because things become tough. It's usually these tough goals that teach us more about ourselves than we would often care to be made aware of.

Use Past Successes

Think about previous achievements and how each of them has made you a better, stronger, more resilient individual. Use each of these factors to lay the foundation for who you are now. This is a starting point for you. Each of these tiny victories we've been talking about could be some of the past successes you can use. Just think that if you have had success once, you can very easily have it again.

Work Consistently

Any goal worth having and worth doing well needs to be performed consistently. You can't take your eye off the ball, not even once. This is one of the reasons why you need to have constant support from those around you–this can be in the form of friends, colleagues neighbors, teachers, and mentors. Even when times are tough, work at achieving your goals both constantly and consistently. If you manage to achieve one goal, it's time to move onto the next one.

One of the most important things to remember as you strive to work consistently on yourself is that you will achieve what you set out to do. You visualize it, work towards it, then it manifests. While this is important, it is even more important to be working on holistic goals to supplement or complement physical goals. This includes your mental, emotional, and spiritual goals. As you pursue these, the vibration you create within yourself will further attract what you desire from your life. You can use height to help you with this. Use your time viewing into the distance as a way to connect to possibility, to connect to what you see yourself attaining, and to create the motivation you need.

Chapter 4:
In the Search of Creativity

"There is no doubt that creativity is the most important human resource of all. Without creativity, there would be no progress, and we would be forever repeating the same patterns."

~ Edward de Bono

The desire to create has also been around since the dawn of time. Long before the grand masters of art, sculpture, and even inventions of the modern age came about, our first parents, and particularly the Egyptians, would keep accurate records of the history of their people inscribed in the walls of the pyramids, inside each of the tombs, and even on top of the sarcophagi.

Each of these inscriptions told a story and created accurate historical records for the people of the time, long before the Rosetta stone took its rightful place as the beginning of actual language. When you consider these ancient monuments that are still steeped in rich historical information today, where archeologists are still only learning to decipher some of the codes and symbols that were used, we can but marvel at the level of creativity that was used.

In modern times, these masters included individuals such as Michelangelo, Matisse, Picasso, and van Gogh to name but a few. Inventors would constantly strive to overcome being tethered to the ground. Consider how the Wright brothers managed to fulfill their desire to solve one of man's biggest challenges—the need to soar, free as the birds above them in the sky.

Far from being the very first to attempt such a feat, Orville and Wilbur Wright remained at it consistently, despite many failed attempts. Did you know that they actually constructed four different aircraft? Each time they failed, they went back to the drawing board and corrected their faults and their flaws and made the next model better than the previous one.

Herein lies the lesson for us that we get to take home from the Wright brothers.

- They weren't the first to attempt to fly; there had been many who had tried and failed.

- Most of the others attempted to fly using what we would today refer to as a paraglider.

- They took their design inspiration from birds that are designed for flight by nature itself. They studied how the birds used their wings to glide in certain directions. This was one of their initial breakthroughs.

Imagine what would have happened if the Wright brothers had insisted on relying on the previous research of all those who had gone before them and failed miserably. They would never have managed to get off of the ground. Instead, they chose to look up and pay close attention to nature instead.

We can each have a similar experience to the Wright brothers. We can spend time in nature waiting, watching, listening, dealing with our thoughts from a deeply introspective situation. Anyone who has a creative bone in their body knows how easy it is to get inspiration directly from nature itself.

This is part of spending time alone on a mountain or a view. It puts life into perspective and can show you things on a much grander scale than if you are at sea level instead. We incorporate our quest for height within ourselves by taking examples of what others have achieved in the field and from nature's example of its own heights. We want to create our own mountain to stand atop—we become the view to look out from, in and of ourselves.

The creative side of the brain and the logical side of the brain form two different hemispheres located side-by-side. This is the difference between those who choose interior design as a field of expertise or accountancy. While it comes across as being a personal preference as to what you enjoy in your life, it is actually whether your left or right brain is dominant.

According to Dr. Robert Shmerling, senior faculty editor at Harvard Health Publishing, approximately 90% of the world's population is right-handed, while only 10% are left-handed. In turn, it's believed that this is a result of brain dominance, being that the left side of the brain controls the right side of the body and vice versa. The left-hand side of the brain deals with logic, reasoning, problem-solving, and technical abilities. The right hemisphere of the brain is more creative and allows for big picture thinking.

Being right- or left-handed, on the other hand, is attributed to genetics more than anything else. Depending on what part of the brain you use, this can determine whether you are more inclined to thinking logically or more creatively (Shmerling, 2019).

There's a very simple trick that you can use in order to get both the right and the left brains talking to one another. This is creating the unique opportunity for both sides of the brain to be working together in harmony with one another. Once you know the secret of being able to activate both sides of your brain simultaneously, you will immediately feel as though you are empowered to create almost anything. The secret is simple. All you have to do at the beginning of each day is to spend a few minutes doodling.

This allows you to use both the logical/cognitive and creative sides of the brain, unlocking both sides, allowing them to communicate with one another. There is also a heightened concentration span, where thought can be controlled to a greater degree.

This singular, simple action seems to put the heart and mind in sync with one another. It allows you to be both logical and creative at the same time. When we are in this frame of mind, we should be able to find connections between ideas that don't seem to be connected at all. Here are a few ways you can improve your ability to become more creative:

Develops Over Time

One of the things that needs to be taken into consideration is that creativity is not something that you suddenly wake up one morning with. Yes, there are people who come across as having a natural talent; they have an eye for detail. Or they know how to mix colors really well. This has all come to them after years of practice and effort. You may need to be especially dedicated in order for these skills and talents to amount to anything that can be applied immediately. As with each of our other skills and talents, there needs to be some failure to facilitate learning in order to be able to grow.

Expand Knowledge

So, you happen to like the work of one particular artist or an era or genre of creativity. How do you expand your current talent, raising the bar by gaining more experience, or improving on your current talent without having to spend years studying? This can usually only be accomplished by extensive studies. The other way is to simply practice. Practice. Practice at every opportunity. Yes, it may mean studying the artist(s) works in great detail, so you get a better idea of specific techniques they have been practicing for years. During this time, try and figure out as much as you can about the artist and their work. This may provide you with some insight into why you find it so magical.

Journaling

This is a great place to start and expand your creative journeys, especially if you are looking to add writing or journaling to your repertoire of skills. If you are going to choose to do this, speaking from experience, every day needs to be filled with writing of some description. Most importantly, when writing by hand, it is very important to write in cursive; it is a lost art, however, very valuable. Further elaborating on journaling from earlier writing will help you put thoughts to paper and manifest your ideas and desires. Affirmations are worth writing down for yourself and reading them daily as a powerful tool.

Sleep More

This is something that I used to be guilty of—not sleeping enough. If you happen to be burning the candle at both ends and are overloaded with work that requires your full mental capacity, you could quite easily suffer from mental fatigue and burnout if you are not careful. I can attest to the fact that good, deep, rapid eye movement (REM) sleep is necessary. You need to be maintaining a regular sleep schedule of between 7-8 hours daily. As you do so, everything is able to improve from there.

Your mental capacity and dream capacity increase, creating a well-rounded effect. Apart from sleeping regularly, being able to dream is extremely important. Find dream supplement herbs if you need to. As you do so, include these dreams in your journal, written in cursive. Do this immediately upon waking, while the memory of the dream is still fresh in your mind. Being able to write these dreams down will help to elevate your level of consciousness and understanding. Let your body and mind get the rest it deserves.

Spend Time with Nature

One of the most effective ways to get in touch with your creative side is by spending time outside and with nature. There is so much beauty in the world to behold. This is especially true when you are doing it from a height that can produce the most amazing sunrise or sunset, or if there's a marvelous view as far as the eye can see. While you are in this space, open your eyes and really look. Take everything in to ensure that you can vividly recall whatever you have seen once you close your eyes. As part of The Process, which we will discuss in Chapter 11, there is a section specifically on being able to recall vivid memories to the fore as and whenever you need them. Nature doesn't have to be a mountain. Perhaps it is a beach, a lake, a waterfall, or a small babbling brook nearby. Ultimately, if none of these are available, then go back to the stargazing technique discussed much earlier on. There you truly are able to get an excellent idea of just how small physically we each are. When you look at things through a global or universal lens, you then come to an understanding that the universe is pondering the same thing looking back at you.

Think Positively

There is definitely power in positive thought, and this is not just a random mantra that was thrown together by Norman Vincent Peale dating back more than half a century ago. This seemed to be proven over and over again by individuals such as Viktor E. Frankl in his epic biography *Man's Search for Meaning,* the classic tribute to hope from the Holocaust.

Very few people connect positive thinking and creativity to creating and living your best life. There are far too many other things that reach the to-do list when it comes to achieving greatness within any field, and creativity never seems to even feature—until now. Even in the worst of times, positive thinking will help. The universe shapes itself around this and materializes your thoughts back at you exactly as you send them out. Negative thinking will only return negative experiences. It is also a matter of perspective. Different people see things differently and not only learn new things, but they also have an opportunity for growth—by using a foundational principle—elevating their thinking.

Think about it for one second. Would you rather have an ivy league graduate on your team that's there for the ride or someone you know who has a solid track record of being able to prove themselves time and time again, as well as being able to solve problems efficiently?

Would you rather have someone who is going to just put their heads down and work, or do you want someone to challenge you because they are hungry for knowledge?

In each of these pursuits, spend quiet time with yourself working through each of these chapters, making notes of things that suddenly spring to your mind as an 'aha' moment. These will be some of the greatest breakthroughs you experience; you will start connecting many moments of your journey as it all comes together before your eyes.

Chapter 5:
In the Search of Spiritual Growth

"The requirements for our evolution have changed. Survival is no longer sufficient. Our evolution now requires us to develop spiritually–to become emotionally aware and make responsible choices. It requires us to align ourselves with the values of the soul– harmony, cooperation, sharing, and reverence for life."

~ Gary Zukav

When it comes to spiritual growth of any description, this is something that is extremely personal. What you would describe as being spiritual for you may not work for your neighbor and so on. This is another thing that makes each of us unique. The other benefit is that we are each free to choose exactly what we believe in, and our spiritual path is ours alone.

It doesn't really matter what you believe in, but fostering and nurturing your inner spiritual/non-physical side is a vital component to being able to grow as a complete individual; this growth touches all aspects of being.

Think for a moment about Orthodox Jews who wear prayer shawls and keep their heads covered. Muslims use prayer mats to pray at specific times of the day. These prayer mats need to be facing the East, and they are encouraged to read from the Quran daily. Christians of all denominations pray and read from the Bible and other books of scripture. Buddhists and Taoists make use of other talismans that form part of their religious ceremonies. We also need to remember those individuals who are not religious but have chosen the spiritual route instead (like myself). We will engage in deep meditation and connect to our Highest Self by aligning our spiritual capacity that way. Through meditation, you can increase your capacity to take in more of what the universe has to offer.

Without using this section to become too specific or to generalize in any singular direction, what we are going to focus on here is creating some form of habit that will allow you to achieve the spiritual growth you are aiming for. Spiritual growth is deeply personal, and I would recommend whether you are religious or not to practice meditation. I cannot begin to explain the massive benefits this has for you.

Set aside time on a daily basis to devote to this practice. This doesn't need to be too long but get into the habit of doing something each day that will strengthen your spirit.

When you think that your spiritual side is a very important aspect to who you are as an individual, then it makes perfect sense that this should be in balance and harmony as much as other areas of your life are. How you choose to do this is completely up to you, but add this to part of your daily routine. We will discuss several topics relating to this a little later when we look at the ways that meditation can benefit your life as a whole. We will cover two specific forms of meditation, one that will become part of your daily routine and the other specific to you whenever you are practicing your meditation in your heightened place.

Let's briefly unpack some different things that you can be doing to improve your spiritual motivation. Some of these include reading from your specific books of scripture or other spiritual material in general. You can broaden your insights and grow further by actually studying in-depth rather than merely glancing over the words hoping that they will find their way deep into the recesses of your mind and your soul.

Physical study is sometimes a lot slower because it is like the word 'study' implies. There is more involved than skimming through a couple of chapters a day. You can set yourself a specific goal that you would like to see achieved within a certain number of months into the future. This may include the number of spiritually aligned or motivational books you plan to study. Studying also requires a pen and paper or notebook where all your insights can be written down. The specific benefits to doing this can prove to strengthen who you are as an individual.

What other spiritual goals do you have that are worthwhile pursuing daily? Maybe this involves discovering your own personal spirit that is within you. This can be done through exercises such as Tai Chi and yoga. The secret to each of these activities is that you do them with the intent to grow and develop in accordance with your Highest Self.

Many religions focus intently on prayer and daily communication, and many spiritual practices have the same focus on meditation depending on your beliefs. Performing these daily is recommended to take advantage of the compounding effect, especially in regards to meditation. Searching inwards through meditation provides you with the opportunity to commune one-on-one with the universe, further allowing yourself to be grateful for the progress you have achieved so far and to ask further for strength to continue.

Set aside specific times to do these things. Another important part of developing yourself spiritually is to make sure that this is a quiet time. Avoid interruptions of any kind. This should be a time where you can be totally quiet, where it's just you and your thoughts, better yet, the lack of thoughts in a state of being one with yourself and the universe. Time for solitude is massively overlooked in today's hyper-connected world; allow yourself to be alone. This time is focused and fully dedicated to nurturing and maximizing your internal growth; focus on raising your consciousness so that you can allow it to be expressed back to you. This way, you gain the most out of this time and experience, opening yourself up to all possibilities.

As you are going through this experience, write down whatever specific or special insights you feel. These can be added to your journal. Often these experiences are extremely spiritual, and you may not want them recorded where anyone can read about them. In this instance, my recommendation is to buy a second notebook or journal and write your spiritual insights in the one that you can keep confidential. The beauty of journaling your spiritual experiences is that they can be read down the road where you can gain additional new insights—and to use this as a support during hard times. I have personally benefited from this exact same process in my life.

I briefly mentioned that you might find that things such as yoga or Tai Chi are beneficial. Dedicate as much time as needed for you to fully benefit from each of these Eastern exercise routines. As we begin to incorporate different methods and spiritual teachings from around the world, we can learn and find gold nuggets of wisdom from each of them and blend them together within ourselves. This allows us to create our own unique perspective and creates a spiritual catalyst for unique expression and path development.

Much of the reasoning behind strengthening your spirit is to be able to control your mind, body, and emotions. You become the master of yourself and not the other way around where you are a prisoner to your mind, body, or emotions.

It's also one of the ways to bring your body back into perfect balance and harmony with the universe, where the choices that you make daily are made from a peaceful space, rather than one that is controlled by the shrill voices that dominate the world today. You are creating a powerful protective spiritual barrier around yourself that strengthens you in good times and times of trials and challenges. If one chooses, my personal experience with enveloping yourself with a golden light shield works very well to dispel negative emotions, mental thoughts, or any other malicious energies.

Chapter 6:
In the Search of Self-Actualization

"Musicians must make music, artists must paint, poets must write if they are to be ultimately at peace within themselves. What human beings can be, they must be. They must be true to their own nature. This need we may call self-actualization."

~ Abraham Maslow

In this section, we are going to discuss exactly what self-actualization is and how it shapes us into the individuals that we are continually striving to be. In keeping with our search of height, the strange thing is that well-known psychologist Abraham Maslow identified what is known as a "hierarchy of needs." The first time this work was ever presented was with one of his scientific papers entitled *A Theory of Human Motivation* which was first published in 1943. This was actually in the shape of a pyramid with the most basic needs at the bottom, working your way up to a state of self-actualization (full elevation).

Let's look at some of these needs and how each of them can apply to us in our lives today:

Right at the bottom of the pyramid, at the base, so to speak, there are all the basic needs that all human beings must have in order to survive. These would include things such as air, water, food, and shelter. These are often referred to as our physiological needs. Think about those things that every living thing needs, and you've pretty much summed up the entire first step (or base) of the hierarchical pyramid.

The second level would include everything needed to feel safe and secure. It needs to be understood that you have to begin building on the bottom before you're able to reach heights that are on another level. So, in this instance, we are assuming that all your physiological needs are being met before considering your safety and security. Your safety includes being safe from war, enjoying financial security, and even having better health. You are probably already beginning to ask yourself whether you have problems in this area; are you stuck? Between your first basic need and your second level of needs, there's a basic shift in what's important when it comes to safety and security.

Once you've been able to check off all the boxes on the second level of the pyramid, the third and center panel is how well you do with your relationships. This could be anyone from your spouse or partner, the neighbors in your community, your family, and friends. How well are you able to connect with them? Do you find communicating with them to be challenging, or do you have loving relationships?

Moving onto the fourth panel, this incorporates how you feel about yourself versus how the world sees you. It's all about your self-esteem. This particular need doesn't stand on its own in isolation. It incorporates other areas of self, including self-confidence, as well as how well you're accepted and treated by those around you.

At the top of the pyramid, the most elevated point, which is actually our topic for this section, is self-actualization. This is your ability to reach your full potential as an individual. The one unique thing about this is that there's no singular way that's correct, and this differs from person to person. Some examples might include achieving a specific goal that you have set for yourself that only you can work on. Once you've achieved this, you've successfully managed to reach a form of self-actualization for that one particular thing. Do you notice that there doesn't seem to be a limit on any of these? You could work at something for a number of months to realize self-actualization in that particular thing, or you may find yourself dedicating your entire life to get there, only to feel that you are failing miserably.

What is also particular to this hierarchy of needs is that when individuals feel as though they are stuck in a rut in one of these five steps, they abandon all hope and simply give up. More often than not, it's usually just before a major breakthrough that people give in, feeling that the achievement in itself is too hard.

Think about this when it comes back to our working from a place where there is great height. Self-actualization is actually at the top (which is where you want to be). You don't want to be messing around in the middle areas of the pyramid, as it is going to hold you back, limit your personal growth and your ability to achieve the heights you've been aiming for in your personal life.

There has been a lot of speculation and debate over this hierarchy of needs, and especially when it comes to self-actualization. According to some experts, self-actualization has more to do with the mindset of someone who is open to growing as an individual rather than having lots of money, being successful, or happy. It's also not believed that because you don't happen to be there right now, you'll never get there. Our lifespans could be long and, during this time, we could fluctuate between these levels.

Several things associated with self-actualization include:

1. In a state of knowing.

2. People have peak experiences.

3. Being creative.

4. Not being biased.

5. Decency.

6. Being able to resolve problems.

7. Enjoy solitude and privacy.

8. They fully enjoy the journey, not just the destination.

Further characteristics that are generally shared by those who achieve self-actualization are as follows:

- They are able to identify what their purpose is and are self-aware.

- They're able to identify what's real and what's not, not only within themselves but also for others.

- They can recognize and appreciate the majesty and wonder in the world around them.

- They have moments of peak experiences on a regular basis. This is something that I am experiencing on a regular basis. It is also the side effect of regular meditation as one works towards raising one's capacity.

- They show compassion and empathy to those around them.

- They are focused on developing solid relationships with those around them.

- They can live independently without having to rely on those around them.

- They have healthy self-respect for themselves and those

around them.

- They have an amazing sense of humor, especially when it comes to finding the lighter side of their own mistakes.

While many believe achieving self-actualization is virtually impossible, there are certain skills that can be learned to help you get there. You may refer to them as possessing a creative spirit.

Some examples of self-actualization include:

- Being confident and secure with who they are.

- Having a great sense of humor even in challenging circumstances. This is especially important during challenging times, more so than in good times.

- Obtaining maximum joy and satisfaction out of every single moment.

- Understanding what was necessary to achieve a sense of accomplishment.

Although at the time Abraham Maslow was convinced that only 1% of the population would ever reach self-actualization, more recent research suggests that figures are currently higher than this. It's felt that one of the key ingredients to achieving self-actualization is being open to growth, and in addition, having the tenacity to do whatever it takes to achieve this growth. This could possibly include your willingness to make sacrifices in order to achieve your goals and so on.

Something that was interesting in this research was that you could actually achieve this state as a temporary measure. Once there, there was no guarantee that you would remain in this state permanently.

The belief that so few individuals would ever achieve this state was purely because it sat at the top of the Maslow pyramid, and not everyone would be able to move through all of the bottom phases. It was also felt that they wouldn't necessarily want to. Some people were perfectly happy being at one level or tier of the pyramid.

The three pioneers of self-actualization were Kurt Goldstein, Carl Rogers, and Abraham Maslow, although the present understanding of self-actualization has adopted the Maslow model rather than following Goldstein and Rogers. According to Maslow, "...the internal drive to self-actualize would seldom emerge until more basic needs are met."

The purpose of this book, however, is to trigger the desire to pursue self-actualization sooner, without having to reach all the necessary requirements on each of the other lower pyramid tiers.

These individuals accept who they are, irrespective of their limitations and personal flaws. They rather relied on their experience and creative drive across all aspects of their lives.

Those who can achieve self-actualization have some common characteristics. They are able to feel and love deeply, despite coming from diverse backgrounds, occupations, and various other differences. They each share loving relationships with people. The self- actualization of more and more people will bring more together, a common bond of consciousness. Everyone has the ability to do this—and a push in the right direction, along with a few tools, will only activate the burning desire towards pursuing the noblest of goals.

This state of joy and ecstasy can also be described as achieving peak experiences as a result of becoming fully developed in appreciating everything that life has to offer; then, because of this appreciation of life, one moves into a state of life themselves.

This can also be achieved when you realize what you are capable of accomplishing. According to Maslow, "Generally, the state of self-actualization is viewed as obtainable after one's fundamental needs for survival, safety, love, and self-esteem are met." (Maslow, 1943, 1954). This is only achieved as you reach your full potential as an individual. Maslow's theory differed in the sense that it was only applicable to human beings rather than to all organisms in the universe.

Self-actualization is when you've been able to achieve your full potential. Very few people reach this aspiration because they are usually working toward achieving more basic goals for survival, and on the other rungs of Maslow's hierarchy of needs. It's our needs that motivate our behavior.

Authors Kendra Cherry and Amy Morin describe self-actualized experiences as being "peak experiences." What do they mean by this? For Maslow, this could only be achieved once each of the other experiences on his pyramid had been achieved; although he believed that the potential was there for anyone to experience self-actualization, he felt that those who had gone through each of the other tiers would be able to experience these more frequently than others.

What does it mean to have a peak experience? These are described as being experiences where you can elevate to experiencing pure joy and elation. While you could often chalk up memorable moments that occurred, these are often described as verging on spiritual experiences—they are that special.

According to author Kendra Cherry, experts that had been spoken to regarding self- actualization describe these experiences as, "Peak experiences involve a heightened sense of wonder, awe, or ecstasy over an experience" (Privette, 2001).

There are three common characteristics of peak experiences:

1. Fulfillment

2. Significance

3. Spiritual

How can we get to experience these peak experiences for ourselves, and how do we know that we are having one of these experiences?

For Maslow, he describes being in love as this type of experience—where you feel that it's one of the best experiences in your life. It's described by experts as being in awe or experiencing extreme happiness and ecstasy.

These don't always need to be connected to your emotions toward someone who is really close to you. You might experience such a profound experience while appreciating a piece of art, listening to a piece of music, and/or looking out at the world from a vast height— literally elevating yourself. It's when something resonates deeply within you on an emotional level, and you feel so moved by it. This can describe how you feel while in this state!

Chapter 7:
In the Search of Inner Peace & Understanding

"The simplification of life is one of the steps to inner peace. A persistent simplification will create an inner and outer well-being that places harmony in one's life."

~ Peace Pilgrim

Almost every day of our lives, there will be situations when we need to be able to tap into a reservoir of peace and calm. This is totally possible for you to achieve by being able to access these calming influences. Depending on who you speak to, peace and understanding could have different meanings to them. Some people may feel that you are referring to peace and understanding on a broader, global level. While this is something that we would all really want—for the world to live in complete peace and harmony continuously—if you're a realist, you will understand that while there may be certain small pockets of peace, it wasn't going to be something that would be long lasting. Global peace is often referred to as a macro-version of peace. We are more interested in the micro- version of peace that comes from each of us internally. It's the peace that we sometimes have to dig deep down for.

Inner peace is something that's very personal and internal. It's the ability to reach deep down within ourselves to achieve a deep and lasting sense of calm and tranquility. From a psychological perspective, the singular definition that they've managed to agree on regarding inner peace is the following as proposed in 2014. "Inner peace refers to a state of being mentally and spiritually at peace, with enough knowledge and understanding to keep oneself strong in the face of stress" (Barabuta, 2014).

Scientists cannot determine whether peace creates happiness or happiness leads to peace. It's a bit like the chicken and the egg. (Which one comes first—peace or happiness?) It may be argued that one can achieve both simultaneously. They do, however, agree that there's a connection between the two.

Here are several ways to increase the peace and harmony levels in your life:

Get Into Nature

There are two specific trains of thought that have been proposed when it comes to spending time in nature. The first is short-term visits in nature, possibly walking or running in a natural environment, leaving all electronic devices and materials at home. The idea is to get out there every day. Keeping within the spirit of this book, natural views offer the motivation and peace one needs.

The second is to spend longer periods in nature for several consecutive days, once again with no interruptions, no media, cell phones, or internet coverage. The longer-term retreats are usually run by companies, departments, religious groups, non-religious groups, and more specific retreat groups. Look for the one that resonates with you the closest before signing up. Even simply go camping for a few days or longer if you desire.

Some additional ways to achieve inner peace are listed below:

Apply the Brakes

I think that you will agree that we all lead pretty hectic lifestyles. We move from one situation to the next, seldom stopping to catch our breath. There are other reasons for slowing down. It can regulate your breathing and your heart rate, particularly if you are feeling stressed. Stress levels can be reduced simply by slowing down the pace of doing things.

Arrive Early

Effective time management skills are essential to developing inner peace. When you're early, you don't waste valuable energy by getting flustered. Arriving early always ensures that you are calm and peaceful when the time comes for your meeting or appointment.

Breathe

Being able to restore balance and harmony to your life can be achieved by practicing some deep breathing exercises. This can be done by taking deep breaths that fill your lungs to capacity. You will know that your lungs are filled to capacity if your stomach feels tight. Hold the breath for a time and slowly release the breath through your mouth. Breathe in through your nose. Practicing these breathing exercises will allow you to reduce feelings of stress and tension that you may be experiencing.

Clear the Clutter From Your Mind

Just as I've recommended cleaning and minimizing the clutter around your workspace, it is just as important to be able to clear the clutter from your mental space. This could be anything from worrying about bills to relationships, your career, finances, and a whole host of other things. We all know that no amount of worrying about something is going to change the outcome. Meditation can be an extremely valuable tool when looking to declutter your mental state.

However, you also need to be able to get rid of the thoughts that are constantly running around your head like a hamster on its wheel, unable to get off. It is believed by scientists that the human brain can process anywhere between 40,000 to 60,000 thoughts in one day. That's a lot of thinking!

Communicate

Too much time and energy are already wasted when we try and guess what someone is saying. When all else fails, communicate directly with the party and ask them what they mean. Often in communication, we leave things to guesswork. We jump to conclusions, and we look at only parts of the picture instead of considering the whole. Is it not just simpler to be upfront and direct from the outset?

If there's something you don't understand, ask for clarification rather than leaving conclusions hanging up in the air. Effective communication requires two parties. Each needs to be given the opportunity to have their say, while the other party should be listening attentively. Anything less than this will result in ineffective communication.

Let Go

One of the biggest challenges we face is learning to forgive, forget, and move on. Even more so is actually letting those things that have happened in the past stay in the past. For many of us, this is a challenge. We claim to forgive, but we battle with the forgetting part. We hold personal grudges against people; instead of being able to move on, this keeps us stuck in the past until we are finally able to release these things, surrendering them to the universe.

Limit Yourself

Much of the stress we feel as individuals is self-inflicted and totally unnecessary. We take on added tasks and responsibilities because we either feel an obligation to someone or we feel as though we are going to be rude if we decline. We need to get out of this habitual behavior as a matter of urgency. There will always be someone who needs our attention or our assistance with something. The problem with not being able to say 'no' results in us becoming totally overloaded and stressed out. This is another unhealthy situation to be in.

Look for Solutions

It's part of human nature to naturally search through whatever is going on in order to identify flaws or errors. Instead of focusing on only those things that happen to be the problem, try and find positives instead. This is like looking for that silver lining around the darkened clouds in the sky. You need to be able to rise above all the shallow drama and the heavy vibrations that permeate through most of society. It is vitally important to raise one's frequency above and beyond all this; it is the equivalent to walking through knee-deep mud without getting dirty.

Pace Yourself

Life is something that is in a constant state of flux, and there always seems to be something that is urgent and in need of our attention. This is just part of life. We need to be realistic in terms of what we can and cannot accomplish within reasonable time frames. Realize you will accomplish everything you set out to do; there is no sense rushing it in regards to universal time. Further, it may be tempting to accept whatever we choose to load on our plates or whatever happens to be loaded there by others. We need to know where to draw the line; it is extremely important not to face burnout purely because we are too afraid of upsetting anyone.

Reduce Stress

Much of this stress could be potentially caused by a similar situation as what is being described above. We need to learn how to reduce the stress that we may be feeling. There are several ways that you can achieve this. Some of them include breaking away from everything for a few minutes, restoring your body to the correct equilibrium and state through the breathing and meditation techniques discussed. You can find ways of becoming physically active to reduce any stress that you may be feeling. This alone can help you clear your mind while restoring and rejuvenating how you feel.

Relax

This is often something that is extremely hard for someone who is constantly busy and productive to have to hear. The reality is that if you don't learn to relax, you are going to end up placing yourself in the firing line of suffering from an emotional or mental breakdown. For you to be able to keep going, you will need to be able to recharge, recuperate, and recover from modern-day stress. This can especially be done by maximizing quality deep sleep. Some of these ways include learning to relax. This could be physically taking a break, being kinder to yourself, not needing things to be absolutely perfect, and occasionally giving yourself a break from it all.

Unplug

Another way to relax is to totally unplug from all forms of social media, the internet, and electronic distractions that could possibly present themselves. This alone can be cathartic. As long as we are connected to social media and we keep on flipping backward and forward between various platforms, subconsciously, we are comparing our lives with those of people that we know who make their lives look glamorous, and they paint the perfect picture for Facebook and Instagram.

Images are photoshopped or presented in the best possible light. This doesn't genuinely represent reality, though. We end up comparing ourselves to some fantasy that has been created for self-promotion. By taking a sabbatical from social media for a couple of days, you will be surprised at how much better you will feel about yourself, as well as the world around you.

Comparing ourselves to others is a complete waste of time and energy. The most important comparison you can make is against yourself—who you were yesterday, who you are today, and the person you would like to become.

Chapter 8:
In the Search of Relieving Mental Health Blocks

"Anything that's human is mentionable, and anything that's mentionable can be more manageable. When we can talk about our feelings, they become less overwhelming, less upsetting, and less scary."

~ Fred Rogers

As we strive to achieve our goals, we are always bound to be facing obstacles, challenges, and failures; it is part of the process and part of life. As we do so, we will discover different ways to relieve and reduce mental health barriers and blocks. These can feel like some of the greatest obstacles we face because they play with us mentally rather than being something tangible that we can actually touch.

In this section, we are going to look at various ways that you can set yourself up to move past each of these barriers, elevating yourself and your life as you do so. Let's get right to it!

Understand that any of us can be facing mental health blocks at any given time; you never know what's going on in the mind of the person next to you. While you see someone who appears to be well-adjusted, well-rounded, and, dare I even say, well-balanced, you never know if they are about to face a complete meltdown. Keep this in the back of your mind as we go through some of the best ways to work through relieving mental health challenges, and as you guessed it, if you can contemplate your mental states from a place of height, you will enhance this process even further.

Choose to Talk Rather Than Bottle

This used to be one of my biggest problems when I was much younger. I would get upset and virtually seethe inside me to the point where I could feel my heart racing almost out of my chest. As far as anyone around me knew, I was cool, calm, and collected as a cucumber. If I hadn't told anyone, none of them would have been any the wiser. They would have just thought I was having an off day. I refused to speak to people about what was going on internally because I saw it as a massive sign of failure.

There was no way that I felt comfortable going to see a mental health practitioner—that was until I was forced to because I could no longer function properly. It was only then that I was referred to someone who specialized in helping individuals cope through stressful situations. The very first thing you must be prepared to do is to talk about whatever is going on in your life, in your mind. Too often, we retort with the response "I'm fine" whenever we are asked how we are coping (especially after a setback). Too often, we are convinced that speaking to someone or even meeting with a certified mental health practitioner is a sign of being a failure.

Know that it isn't. You are actually choosing to do one of the most difficult things possible, but you aren't just doing it for you; you're doing it for your loved ones and all those around you too. Nobody can support you if they don't know what you're going through. Now I'm not saying that you switch over completely to being surrounded by unnecessary drama for the sake of drama. Even if you are in the midst of the drama, there are certain things that you do keep confidential and just between you and your mental health practitioner.

It is also important to not pass all of your toxic problems onto others, especially if they are not ready to listen. This drains energy rather than creating it. Work with those you are talking with to find solutions. Remain positive and know that everything will work itself out.

That's the reason for choosing to meet with a mental health practitioner in the first place. If you feel that you can no longer do this on your own, look for someone who can just listen to you while you unburden some of those things that you may have been carrying around with you for a long time.

Something that works for me is talking with myself about my problems. If you can do this while staring off into the distance from a height, you can visualize the problems disappearing with gravity and falling away down into the vast expanse. This can also be done by looking at the stars or the sky. It is a powerful form of self-therapy.

Follow Your Passion

Find something that you really enjoy doing and do it, even if it's to break the monotony of your normal routine. Consider something that you haven't done in ages, but you are passionate about. Maybe it's drawing, or painting, or writing, fly fishing, or horseback riding. Let your imagination run wild. Don't stop yourself from considering various different options. You want to be able to have the creative freedom necessary for you to be able to unwind completely. It may even be a great idea to switch your electronic devices off and simply unplug for a day where you don't need to worry about whether you are doing the right thing or not. Give yourself a pass for the day.

Give Yourself a Breather

Stop and take a 5-minute breather. Remember that you are an infinite consciousness having a human experience; however, our physical bodies have certain limitations. We can only keep going for so long without having a break. Give yourself permission to slow down and relax whenever it is necessary—even if this is just long enough for you to be able to recharge your batteries. We all need time where we can unwind. This is a perfect time for you to elevate yourself physically and visit your mountain.

Love Yourself

This is another very challenging thing to learn to do. We are always so critical of and so hard on ourselves. We constantly compare ourselves to those who are either closest to us or those within our social network sphere of influence. We compare ourselves to them by taking into constant consideration that we will never be able to live up to their standard. The point is, why would we want to be exactly the same as someone else in the first instance? We should learn to be content with ourselves; however, we should still strive for improvement and, most importantly, love ourselves. Love will not come to you otherwise.

Take Care of Yourself

When it comes to this, it encompasses a whole host of things. Looking after yourself includes your diet, sleep routine, physical activities, meditation, and small but important things like drinking enough water throughout the day. Don't isolate yourself from the rest of the world. Be sure to make regular arrangements to meet up with close friends, family, or other relatives. Spend quality physical time with them. It has become way too easy to use technology to get in touch with people instead of making use of other methods at your disposal.

Set a coffee date and then follow through by actually being there. Allow yourself to open up to your friends and family, so they know what's going through your mind, and also in order for them to identify when you are in trouble. Identify one or two very close friends or family members to be your sounding boards that if you are really feeling down, you can make contact with them and just talk. You have no idea just how cathartic being able to talk and having someone to listen can be.

Whenever you find yourself in trouble, don't be too afraid to ask for help. The adage that "no man is an island" rings true in this instance. Once you've asked for help, allow them to help you. Often we half-heartedly ask for help without really wanting people to get too close to the situation. In this instance, let your support system in.

We finally need to realize that the act of taking care of ourselves is very important if we desire to help others around us. Your foundation needs to be strong, as your example is what lights the way for anyone that may need help. What good are you if you cannot even take care of yourself? Further, who will want to help you if you do not even want to help yourself?

Chapter 9:
In the Search of Relieving Stress, Anxiety & Indecision

"Within you, there is a stillness and a sanctuary to which you can retreat at any time and be yourself."

~ Hermann Hesse

Anxiety and stress can lead to poor decision-making. One of the ways that it does this is by ensuring that we always err on the side of caution when making decisions. While this can often protect us, it can also keep us from living the best life possible. If we are constantly only making those decisions that are safe, we could miss out on a lot of opportunities that could lead to a much better life for ourselves and those around us.

Staying safe all the time will not push you out of your comfort zone. You will stagnate and get used to it unless some dramatic event brings about rapid change. Safety can also be seen as doing things that don't rock the boat; however, where's the fun in that? To elevate yourself to your fullest potential, you will have to engage in unsafe things—not unsafe in a physically harmful way, but by doing things that will test you physically, mentally, and spiritually even to the point where you can experience discomfort at times. Only then can you build on these experiences to greater heights.

Anxiety and Decision-Making

According to research, anxiety can disengage an area of the brain that helps us make sound decisions. This area is known as the prefrontal cortex (PFC).

Without the prefrontal cortex being able to calm the decision-making process, most decisions are made out of fear which is based on raw emotions instead of rational thinking. The PFC calms the amygdala, which is responsible for creating fear within us. We need to be able to think rationally, logically, weighing up all the pros and cons when making decisions.

Anxiety causes distractions and disruptions, which prevent the rational side of the brain from making the best possible decision. There are ways to prevent intrusive thoughts from inhibiting correct decision-making, and these include:

Become Calm

By taking your time to learn how to slow down, you can become more aware of your thoughts and feelings that are involved in the decision-making process. It may sound easy to slow down your thought process. In truth, this is a lot more difficult than it may sound. Making decisions is something that we often do on a subconscious level. By becoming calm, you can slow down enough to be able to see things as they are, rationally.

Challenge Thinking

It would be worthwhile for you to develop the ability to challenge each of those thoughts that cross your mind. This is almost an extension of mindfulness—being able to examine the thoughts and emotions that you have and then applying critical thinking. In order to apply critical thinking, you need to be able to clear your mind of all distractions. These distractions stop us from being able to apply logic to the decisions we need to make.

Decide on What You Want

We are often drawn toward making decisions based on what we don't want rather than waiting and trying to figure out exactly what we do want. This should be adjusted, so we make wiser decisions. When you are indecisive or make your decision out of fear, this decision is not necessarily the right one. Indecision, in a way, is a decision; however, it is better to make a decision and fail than to live a life of regret thinking, "What if?"

Don't Be Afraid of Wisdom

When we make decisions from a place of clarity and wisdom, then the chances are that we are making a decision that is going to be in our best interest. Acquire this wisdom within yourself through your meditative practices. This access to knowledge is a birthright of all that make an effort to pursue it.

Identify Anxiety

Figure out exactly where your stress and anxiety are coming from. Are you anxious about work, home life, relationships, things that have happened in the past that suddenly resurface? If you know where your stress is coming from, it can become easier to manage.

Mindfulness Exercises

Practicing mindfulness techniques can allow you to regain control of the PFC. When the PFC is compromised, rational decision-making becomes that much harder when you're anxious. By being mindful, you can train the brain to become stronger in reducing these distractions, making decisions easier.

Not All Choices Are Bad

Occasionally we prevent ourselves from making decisions or choices because we're too afraid of making the wrong decision. While this is an admirable trait to develop, we need to remember that not all choices are bad. You can find yourself in a situation where you happen to make the wrong decision; however, this is not the end of the world. You can still learn a tremendous amount to use moving forward; this is how "bad decisions" are turned into good learning outcomes. This is where the beauty of decision-making comes into play, that you have the ability to be able to change the decisions you make, to believe, and eventually to 'know' there are better options available to you.

Think, Feel, Act

You may believe that with all thought processes, we need to follow through with the triangle of thinking, feeling, and then choosing to act. This is not true. Not every thought process has to follow this pattern. We know from being able to practice mindfulness that you can allow a thought to simply be a thought that drifts in and out of your head—nothing more, and nothing less. Because you think something doesn't mean that you automatically need to pay any specific emotions to it or that you need to act on it.

Procrastination

Whenever we battle with decision-making as a result of being unsure of ourselves, the result is further stress. This can lead to fear. One of the ways we deal with these fears is by procrastinating. We would rather not make any decision at all rather than a wrong decision, but fear of making this decision is what holds us back. So, how can you learn to overcome this?

Situations that we face daily can leave us spinning our wheels rather than trying to find the best answer to some of life's most challenging questions. Things like,

- What is my main purpose on earth?
- What should I do with my life?
- Who should I be listening to regarding what to do after college?
- Should I even go to college?

There are some effective ways to learn to overcome a procrastination habit. These include:

- Don't be afraid to make a decision just because you don't have all the facts. You will gain more and get to see the big picture only once you become fully immersed in the situation.
- Figure out a way to plan how, when, and where you will act. Remember that you don't need to have everything figured out just yet. You can revise, review, and reinvent your plan as you receive additional information.

- Weigh all the options, especially anything negative that could stand in your way. One of the easiest ways to overcome genuine fear is by confronting it head-on. Consider the following, and don't be afraid to review and revise your answers to each situation. "What is the worst that can happen?" Once you know this, you can begin to prioritize which of your current situations need to be closely monitored for proof that what you have assumed to be true is, in fact, true.

You can begin to search for each of these answers in quiet times as you elevate yourself physically, spiritually, and emotionally. Remember to make use of your journal for any important impressions or insights that you may be feeling.

In the next parts, we are going to look at the way that these things can be beneficial to us, as well as considering The Process behind The Unleashing Your Full Potential.

Chapter 10:
In the Search of Confidence & Self- Awareness

Building Confidence

Self-confidence is not something that comes automatically to everyone. As a matter of fact, none of us are actually born with an endless supply of self-confidence. It is something that we need to develop. Being able to develop self-confidence is possible, but it also takes a lot of self-belief. We need to know that we are going to push ourselves toward reaching our goals harder than we have done ever before.

According to E. E. Cummings,

"Once we believe in ourselves, we can risk curiosity, spontaneous delight, or any experience that reveals the human spirit."

Is this not what we all want to experience? As much as what we are able to do or push ourselves to do that is within our personal capacity as human beings?

What then is holding us back from this achievement? There is a single word that springs to mind that will hold us back every single time—fear. We can allow this fear to engulf us and keep us from reaching our full potential. There are so many ways that this single emotion can totally take over our lives and prevent us from moving forward.

I don't care who you are. At some stage of your life, you will be crippled by this emotion. The question that is then asked is how you can overcome this fear that is stopping you from achieving your goals and objectives. It can easily paralyze you in the moment, to the point where you choose to rather do nothing than at least attempt to do something while not realizing that choosing to do nothing is still a choice, one that the consequences for can be more dire than making a "wrong choice."

Is it better to at least attempt to do something and fail, or is it better not to do anything at all?

We start off with self-awareness, but in order to develop the understanding, we need to grow our self-esteem and confidence. Further, you as an individual have a tremendous capacity to achieve greatness. You need to take the chance on yourself because no one else will.

Here are some of the things that could help increase your self-confidence. In some instances, people separate each of these into different categories. While in some ways they can be slightly different, they are actually interchangeable and connected to one another. This is where our focus is going to be for the remainder of this section. Realize too that self-confidence is the process of elevating yourself within; as this happens, confidence grows, your output grows, and your total being manifests before your eyes, slowly but surely.

Creating Confidence

"Somehow I can't believe that there are any heights that can't be scaled by a man who knows the secrets of making dreams come true. This special secret, it seems to me, can be summarized in four Cs. They are curiosity, confidence, courage, and constancy, and the greatest of all is confidence. When you believe in a thing, believe in it all the way, implicitly and unquestionably."

~ Walt Disney

Here are some examples that can help you develop your confidence. However, understand that it starts with the desire to build yourself up from whatever position you may find yourself in currently.

Be Grateful

This is definitely a habit worth developing. It doesn't even need to take a lot of time out of your day—a small morning or evening meditation will do. The power of gratitude is that the more you are grateful for, the more the universe will give you to be grateful for.

Be Kind and Approachable to Others

The world needs a whole lot more kindness and consideration toward others, in essence, treating others as you want to be treated. You know how uncomfortable it can be when you are trying to work with individuals that come across as being completely shut off from the world. It really isn't fun at all. Ensure that you don't slip into this category accidentally.

Be Prepared

I mentioned above that we are often fearful because we forget to prepare ourselves to face something. This is exactly the same as being prepared for a presentation, handing in an assignment or test, or even taking a follow-up call with a customer. When you are prepared, you can be more confident within yourself.

Change One Small Habit

Think about one small habit that you can change, adopt, or implement as part of your daily routine. Maybe you're one of those people who like to keep on hitting the snooze button over and over again each day. Set yourself a goal to get up when the first alarm goes off. You may need to improve your daily intake of healthy foods. In this instance, pack a healthy meal for lunch rather than relying on ordering from your favorite deli. You are not looking at changing the entire world here or all at once. You are looking at changing one micro-habit at a time. Set yourself a goal to stick with for between 30-45 days because by then, you can be sure that it has become a habit.

Clear Clutter From Your Workspace

It's difficult to explain the negative impact that clutter and chaos can have on your ability to be productive. If you know that your workspace is cluttered, then look at making changes to get rid of what is distracting you. While on this topic, it also applies to keeping your workspace clean and dust-free. You will be amazed at how different you feel once your work area is neat, clean, and fresh. It will give you an amazing sense of power and organization to work from.

Dress Like You Mean Business

There's an old adage, and I give credit where it is due that goes something like this: "Get up, dress up, and show up!" This is such a powerful short statement to live by. If you know that you have a problem with working in sweats or your pajamas all day long because you are working remotely and have no physical interaction with people, then this is especially for you. I can promise you that when you dress like you mean business, you will suddenly feel like you are in "business mode."

Establish Principles to Live By

Having principles and rules to live by is something that is vitally important for success. You want people to like and trust you because this is one of the first rules of business. Successful people will only be drawn toward you if you have a high set of moral standards and principles that you have established for yourself and you're living by them.

Exercise

To keep the mind healthy and body healthy, exercising and ideally staying in peak physical condition is necessary. Use this foundation to maintain health for yourself and your ability to tackle life's problems. You can make this one of your small habits that you try and crack, even if it's for just 5 minutes a day. That 5 minutes will eventually compound, and you could find yourself even adding to it with greater intensity.

Finish Something You've Been Procrastinating About

I think that to some degree or another, we all suffer from procrastination. In order to get moving, look at some of the tasks that you have been holding off for whatever reason and decide to tackle just one of them. Do whatever you have to do in order to get the job done. Start off small once again. Set aside 20-30 minutes where there will be no interruptions, just focused attention at seeing how many of these semi-finished or totally neglected tasks can be finished. As you manage to complete each of these items, scratch them off of your to-do list. There is something that is psychologically satisfying at seeing certain things being marked off of a list. It will actually get you motivated to keep going.

Get Going

This is closely interlinked with procrastination and the entire section above. We often make tons of excuses why we cannot do something; the circumstances aren't just perfect, the planets aren't aligned—whatever the reason, we have probably found most of them at some time or another. The secret to overcoming procrastination is to just get going. As an author, there's always the excuse of having "writer's block" where I can stare blankly at a page for ages before receiving a sudden burst of information that can then be captured on a page. To be honest with you, not doing something is possibly just an excuse and something that should be ignored as an excuse.

Get Small Things Out of the Way First

Get into the habit of working on the small things first. Tackle each of those tasks that can easily be tackled within a few minutes, whether making a couple of quick phone calls, typing out a couple of ideas for a new novel, or working through your emails. There is no particular order that these tasks need to be accomplished in, but the most important thing is that they get done, get marked off, and get out of the way. Once you get into the habit of getting small things out of the way first, you will never go back to procrastinating ever again.

Learn Something New

Knowledge is power, and this is true at any age. When we believe that we have all the knowledge we need, we are standing on a very slippery slope indeed. We are never too old to discover new skills or sharpen techniques and problem solving through additional knowledge. Set yourself a target or a goal to learn at least one new thing every day of your life (as simple as reading one new bit of information). The compounding factor will come into play. By the end of a year, you will have learned almost 400 new things.

Look For Solutions Rather Than Problems

This is the difference between optimism and pessimism. You have the choice about what you choose to see. Those around you don't enjoy it when all that the person sees are problems. Yes, it may be challenging, and you may have to look for creative ways to come up with solutions, but that's what part of this process is all about—discovering the creativity that's deep within you.

Set and Work Toward Achieving Small Goals

Your goals don't need to be monumental accomplishments. Instead, look for small, bite- size goals that can be achieved within a reasonable amount of time. It's important that these goals be manageable because the success of these will motivate you and drive you toward the achievement of bigger and brighter things.

Smile

Something as simple as being friendly toward those that you come across can increase your confidence. People will treat you with respect and different from those that are miserable all the time. You will also feel happier within yourself and about the future prospects of your life if you can exude a degree of confidence by smiling. The other thing about a smile is that it costs nothing.

Speak With Confidence

Speaking with confidence will sometimes require loads of practice, especially if you don't like crowds or speaking in front of a lot of people. One of the ways to do this is by speaking a lot slower than you normally would. Be sure to articulate your words correctly so that people can understand you. Some of the biggest mistakes that individuals make are speaking too quickly, swallowing their words, not making eye contact, and mumbling.

Stand Taller

This can tie in with being able to speak with confidence. There's something about making yourself stand taller that automatically makes you seem to be larger than life. You will automatically feel more confident just by making a small adjustment to your posture.

Stop Negative Thoughts in Their Tracks

The second you realize that you are beginning to have any negative thoughts about yourself, a situation, or something that you're involved with, it's important to try and catch them and squash them immediately. The best way to get rid of negativity is by replacing it with both thoughts and actions that are positive.

Meditation

Meditation will be the ultimate foundation to build your confidence up from; it will allow you to center yourself within this world as a whole and the world around you that you directly experience. The sense of knowing where you are and how you are doing is confidence; this trust in yourself will be unbreakable and enduring.

Initial Benefits

"Infuse your life with action. Don't wait for it to happen. Make it happen. Make your own future. Make your own hope. Make your own love. And whatever your beliefs, honor your creator, not by passively waiting for grace to come down from upon high, but by doing what you can to make grace happen... yourself, right now, right down here on Earth."

~ Bradley Whitford

There are amazing benefits to be gained from observing the world, the heights to achieve within yourself, assisted by the heights you have scaled to achieve them from. Contemplate this. As the higher you go, the more your feelings will be magnified. This is one of the reasons why stargazing is so powerful. You are staring into space, at the stars, possibly the furthest you can go, looking outward from the ground, toward the vast reaches of the heavens. This can be done either during the day or at night; however, at night, you get a much clearer scale of the expansiveness of the universe and everything it has to offer you.

It is recommended that these exercises be done on your own. Much of the time spent focusing on the vista or vast expanse before you will give you the much-needed peace, silence, and solitude for you to be able to get to know who you are as an individual. It provides you with the chance to develop your meditative qualities, experience your own existence, and nurture feelings of peace and general well-being as a whole.

During this time, you can experience insights that are out of this world and beyond the horizon. This expanded worldview allows the depth of understanding to grow your consciousness. It will let you simply enjoy what you are looking at and acting in—the entire world before your eyes.

Benefits

The key benefits that you can enjoy from these experiences have a direct influence on many areas of your life. I have separated these into several major categories and will expand on each of these individually. The first of these are:

Spiritual:

Meditation

During this time, you are at one with the environment, at one with yourself, and at one with the expanse before your eyes. This is your space where there is nothing but you and the universe. Nothing can distract you; experience for yourself truly an eyes open meditation simply by staring at the scene in front of you. Take it in, empower yourself.

This process of elevating physically allows higher states of consciousness to flow in, higher states of mental functioning, and higher states of connection to it all to envelope your entire being. A true sense of self-actualization is achieved, that peak experience is possible, and anything is within reach.

Before our eyes, we see the big picture—of the view and in life—our purpose is more fully visible, and our drive to develop and grow burns bright. These qualities are and can be achieved from meditation alone; however, I would like for you to add the elevation process to help simplify what internally can be done. To eliminate feeling small about yourself, to eliminate anything that is standing in the way of your search of height.

Mental:

Mental benefits we enjoy through these elevation techniques include receiving inspiration and creative ideas. This is the root of ways to solve problems that we may currently be dealing with. This comes through the power of thought and being able to take the initial concept, idea, problem, or experience that you may be having and processing each of these in creative ways. You need to be able to understand problems holistically where you can get the big picture of a situation to be able to mentally conquer any troubles and attain the knowledge that you can.

Emotional:

Here you find true peace and tranquility. Allow this to boost your self-confidence, especially if you happen to be afraid of heights. Let it provide you with an opportunity to relieve yourself from anxiety, stress, and depression. You have a chance to consider that there are others out in the world who have greater problems than you feel you have.

The physical sensations that you get when you are that elevated can make you feel like you want to fly. Fly within, fly with your mind, fly with your consciousness. Feel the experience of being grounded yet still elevated within yourself.

In Unleashing Your Full Potential is all about the whole human experience. It is about elevating oneself and others along the way as you journey through life. There is a complete evolution that begins to take place within you holistically as an individual. Consider each aspect of your life as part of who you are because they all form part of your makeup as a human being.

Some of these areas include:

Physical:

Think about ways that you can elevate your physical health. This could be anything from working on an exercise routine to eating correctly. For some people, it may even be as simple as trying to break a bad habit by replacing it with something that is more beneficial to your health. Small and simple changes can make a major difference in your life. All you need to do is be willing to start and continue on your path of growth. Do what you can, do it consistently, even add intense exercise into your routine, or something as simple as long walks; nevertheless, make physical growth a part of your total plan to pursue your development.

Knowledge:

When it comes to knowledge, we are told that it is power. This is true. We can acquire as much knowledge as we want to elevate ourselves into that higher intelligence state. According to genius scientist Albert Einstein, he said that "Anyone can become a genius by applying themselves just 10 minutes daily for a year." Think about that for a second. If you really want to know something bad enough, and you were willing to apply just 10 minutes to the subject matter for a year, you will see the compounding effect of all that knowledge being accumulated.

I know that for most of us we will battle to become another Einstein, or maybe that's not the goal for us—maybe the goal is to become better at a specific skill that will assist us in the workplace. Whatever it is, if you decide that you are going to go after something and you want it badly enough, you can easily elevate your knowledge and the power that comes with it by breaking things down into bite-size chunks. These are definitely more manageable than trying to cram something into your brain over a longer period of time.

Finances & Career:

What about your financial health? How can you elevate your financial status? This is a question that's often asked because, let's face it, without money, it's difficult to live. We all would battle to survive without having the financial means to pay for our very basic needs. Consider Maslow's hierarchy of needs. If we cannot afford even the very basics on that list, food, clothing, and shelter, how do we expect to progress and move ourselves forward financially, let alone towards self-actualization?

When it comes to our financial health, are we setting aside a certain amount of our income every month? Are we working within a reasonable budget? Do we know where our money is going every month, or do we just spend randomly? What is our credit score like? Do we even know what a credit score is and why it's important? More importantly, are we striving to perform our best at whatever job we are employed in?

When it comes to working any job or your career, it is important to do the best you can to always look for efficiencies and ways you can improve and improve the company. These very strong habits and work ethic will contribute to your financial health in ways you cannot even begin to imagine. As you develop in the workplace, opportunities to apply for promotions come up. Without working hard, these become missed, and stagnation in the workforce follows. Always keep your eyes open for better jobs and apply, believe in yourself, and consistently improve your skills in fields such as negotiation, people skills, and selling; all three in different and combined ways are very important in any business workplace situation.

Moving on, we consider many aspects of development; yes, having financial freedom is a very noble goal. I would recommend working on your whole self, physically, mentally, and spiritually. Developing these areas will help you attract and work on the financial situation you desire, further contributing to an overall fully elevated life.

Chapter 11:
In the Search of The Process

"Twenty years from now you will be more disappointed by the things that you didn't do than by the ones you did do. So throw off the bowlines. Sail away from the safe harbor. Catch the trade winds in your sails. Explore. Dream. Discover."

~ Mark Twain

Explore, dream, discover—beautiful words to describe the elevation process; in fact, the whole path of self-development is a lifelong discovery into what you can achieve as you explore life and work towards your dreams. The whole seacrh of height has a strong emotional component; the entire process is about looking out to see the whole playing board in front of your eyes, so let yourself be amazed by the beauty of it all. See things as though you were an eagle soaring over a vast plain, observing everything that is happening below. Allow this perspective to fill your entire being.

During your first stage, as you adventure out to seek the heights upon which to stand, have this process be a deliberate effort that you are making towards improving your life and striving for something better. Getting to the destination that you choose is going to inspire a certain degree of adventure deep within you.

The adventure begins in trying to identify what will become your specific "high spot." If you don't live in a mountainous region, then look for some high-rise buildings where you can get access to a viewing deck and/or use stargazing as a powerful option. Once there you spend enough time alone, just with the view, this is the very first stage of achieving new heights.

As you experience the height, allow yourself to find inspiration and to contemplate where you are and where you intend to go; use the moment to fill your being with the energy you need to strengthen your resolve. This process of taking it all in is your second stage. With this, your motivation will grow, your path to self-actualization will be shown, and any mental restraints will be eased and lifted as you realize there are much greater concepts to focus on, to use, to understand.

This is where the adventure of life really begins.

After soaking it all in, after filling your being with inspiration, begin the process of looking inwards. I recommend using meditation, look to find the peace and strength inside, know it, feel it—this is what elevation inside you is. Allow yourself to be grateful for the moment and everything that comes to you. These emotions that envelope you are used as the fire to visualize your future and what you will accomplish, seeing it clearly with focus. This is the third and final stage of the search of height. Everything else falls into place.

This practice is an ongoing addition to your life. As you grow more and develop, you will want to continue this process to contemplate your progress; use the solitude to be with your growth. Further inspire yourself with what you have accomplished. The heights you choose to gaze from will be a reflection of where you want to go in life. Propel yourself towards your elevated future.

Conclusion:
Achieved Height

"Men go abroad to wonder at the heights of mountains, at the huge waves of the sea, at the long courses of the rivers, at the vast compass of the ocean, at the circular motions of the stars, and they pass by themselves without wondering."

~ Saint Augustine

By practicing and incorporating the various techniques outlined throughout the book, we begin and/or continue to achieve our very best selves. Through our reflection of the whole process, we realize that we are much greater than we ever thought possible; we realize our potential and bring forth our sense of wonder towards our search of height. This pursuit, as said before, is a noble pursuit, one which we will win. I would like to share an inspirational quote with you to help bring the search of height into further perspective:

"We choose to go to the moon in this decade and do the other things, not because they are easy, but because they are hard, because that goal will serve to organize and measure the best of our energies and skills, because that challenge is one that we are willing to accept, one we are unwilling to postpone, and one which we intend to win, and the others, too."—J.F. Kennedy

May this inspire you to take upon the challenge that you are willing to accept to pursue the vast heights within yourself. We sometimes just need the right view or the right thing said to put things into perspective for us, to be able to see clearly and far, to be able to access and assess the bigger picture worth going after. It's like having an entire territorial map open that shows the areas all around you versus just having a small, local section open. You will never achieve your goals or dreams without first specifying them to yourself, without accepting that you will pursue that direction, without receiving the necessary inspiration you need from within and from the world around us—allow a place of high elevation to assist you with this inspiration.

There is magic that happens within us. We can translate the things we learn about ourselves, about our goals, about the world around us, about our hopes, and about our dreams into future achievements and into the wisdom we need for the application of our all-out effort towards the self-actualization of our physical, mental, emotional, and, above all, spiritual capacities.

If you have already been successful in achieving many of these things listed and what your heart desires, then being in a position of height, assessing yourself from this will give you the ability to understand more about who you are as an individual. Use this to consolidate where you have been, the road that you traveled on to get here, and the gratitude for each of the things that you have. May this help you even further develop your life to its fullest potential, may that determination to grow never cease to exist. And for anyone that is just beginning their adventure of life, their first steps to achieving growth, or those that are already well along the road of self-development, may you continue to find the strength, courage, and determination to never yield in the face of adversity, to never yield to doubt, to never yield to settling for mediocrity. May this fire burn bright and long, through day and night, during your search of height!

Author's Note

Dear Reader,

Thank you for purchasing my book and taking the time to read through the material. I hope you received as much enjoyment from it as I did writing it. May you take from it a new sense of direction and purpose towards striving for your own personal growth.

I would like to take this time to humbly ask that you leave me an honest review on whatever platform you purchased this book from. I do take the time to read all of them to further assist me in my growth and to make improvements to my published works. This would be greatly appreciated, and I offer you my sincerest gratitude for taking the time to leave a review for me.

May we all achieve our fullest potential and then push even further. And so, it is.

Most Gratefully Written, Emily.

Unleashing Your Full Potential!
EMILY KENDALL

© Copyright 2021 - All rights reserved.

....

The content contained within this book may not be reproduced, duplicated or transmitted without direct written permission from the author or the publisher.

Under no circumstances will any blame or legal responsibility be held against the publisher, or author, for any damages, reparation, or monetary loss due to the information contained within this book. Either directly or indirectly.

Legal Notice:

This book is copyright protected. This book is only for personal use. You cannot amend, distribute, sell, use, quote or paraphrase any part, or the content within this book, without the consent of the author or publisher.

Disclaimer Notice:

Please note the information contained within this document is for educational and entertainment purposes only. All effort has been executed to present accurate, up to date, and reliable, complete information. No warranties of any kind are declared or implied. Readers acknowledge that the author is not engaging in the rendering of legal, financial, medical or professional advice. The content within this book has been derived from various sources. Please consult a licensed professional before attempting any techniques outlined in this book.

By reading this document, the reader agrees that under no circumstances is the author responsible for any losses, direct or indirect, which are incurred as a result of the use of information contained within this document, including, but not limited to, — errors, omissions, or inaccuracies.

....
Thank you for buying this book.

www.ingramcontent.com/pod-product-compliance
Lightning Source LLC
Chambersburg PA
CBHW031125080526
44587CB00011B/1110